Reboot!

Your Working Relationships

Marcia Feola

ISBN: 1-4392-2654-7
ISBN-13: 9781439226544

Visit www.amazon.com to order additional copies.

Contents

Reboot! | Introduction

Today is the age of partnerships, teams and true collaboration—which means that how we lead must change. The new leadership model is about learning how to cooperate instead of compete, share instead of hoard, create harmony instead of discord.

This book is for the new leader. Specifically, it is for the leader who needs to address discord in the workplace. It offers a guide to having conversations that explore and resolve conflicts. And in doing so, it shows leaders how to reboot relationships and get back on track to successful work by naturally aligning your needs with those of your co-workers.

Human relationships are full of complexities. Many a book has been written on the topic of human dynamics in hopes of improving human interactions. In business literature much has been written on motivation, emotional intelligence and leadership—all in the hopes of making our organizations more humane and more productive. This book has been written with the same hope of elevating human interactions, improving our work environments and achieving organizational success.

The idea for *Reboot!* comes from my deep belief that we all want to have a positive impact on this world and that we all come to our work and to our relationships with positive intentions. If we dialogue well, listen deeply and tell our individual truth, we will be able to see a situation more fully, create more possibilities and find new and better ways of working.

Reboot! does not attempt to analyze or explain human development or human dynamics. It simply outlines a process for having the type of conversation that can transform a strained relationship or situation into an opportunity to grow, learn and start anew. Please note that, while I refer to "co-workers" throughout the text, this type of conversation can occur between any members of an organization—especially between you, as a manager, and your subordinates.

Welcome to the new conversation: ***Reboot!***

"It's not what life throws at you. It's how you deal with it that matters."

—Gladys Melamed, my mother

1 | Conflict is normal.
Step into it, not away from it.

Wherever we go and whatever we do, we inevitably hit bumps, turns, surprises and mysteries. Our journeys unfold in many different ways. Such is the fabric of life. Our organizational lives are the same way.

As leaders and managers, our work requires interface and connectivity to others. How we deal with obstacles and challenges is what makes the difference. Taking what we commonly think of as hard or uncomfortable moments with co-workers or subordinates and turning them into opportunities to explore, grow and be creative is the key to building solid relationships and getting work done well. Ignoring these opportunities to "reboot" our relationships will only lead to poor work and, possibly, a descent into more painful conflicts.

John Sherwood's seminal Pinch Model of conflict resolution illustrates quite well how relationships are formed as people join an organization, and how conflict—or "pinches"—can enter those relationships.

Initial entry: This is the period early in a hiring process or introduction to a new job or assignment. During this phase information is shared among managers and co-workers and expectations are negotiated.

Commitment: This phase comes after roles have been clarified and expectations are clear. People begin working, a level of commitment is established and stability is apparent.

Disruption: As work progresses, something inevitably changes in the relationship. The cause of the change could be any number of factors: people grow, customer demands change, competitors enter the scene, the environment puts a strain on the company, someone encounters personal problems. For whatever reason, there is a "pinch" or, as I call it, a "moment" when we realize that things are not going well.

For the purpose of this book, a pinch is defined as a sense of discomfort or unease. It's the earliest sign of disequilibrium in a relationship, and it typically starts with negative personal feelings. You might feel unhappy, frustrated, disappointed or just uneasy. However you recognize that something is amiss, a pinch is the first moment you realize that you are not satisfied with someone you interact with at work. And that pinch, or moment, is the very best time to stop and examine your relationship.

Why? Because overlooking or ignoring the sense that something isn't going well with a relationship usually leads to the situation worsening, and to the development of a more strained relationship or a true conflict. The best course of action is to take notice of your feelings and reactions.

Also, pay attention to what you are thinking or saying. Are you wondering why work isn't going well? Are you theorizing why a co-worker isn't doing her job well? Are you sitting in judgment of yourself or others? Do you find yourself avoiding someone or having to withhold expressing your dissatisfaction? These are "moments"—and they are hallmarks of a situation that requires a conversation.

At this point in the life cycle of work there is an opportunity to reboot the relationship and examine the situation with an eye toward improving it. Paying attention to when these moments appear and stepping into them, not away from them, will change your working relationships and increase your work success.

Because confrontations like these are often dreaded, however, many managers deal with them ineffectively. Yet, as John Sherwood explains, these moments are to be expected. And seeing conflict as normal is the first step in being able to approach it with thoughtfulness and openness.

This is where "how you deal with it" comes in. Taking the "ignore-it-and-it'll–go-away" route rarely works. More often the situation gets worse...and then it HURTS! You can remedy a situation when it reaches that "pain point," but by then the conflict takes longer, has more baggage to clean up and is harder to repair. The best opportunity to remedy the situation is at the start, during the pinch point.

These moments are, in fact, an opportunity to learn, grow and be creative. They look scary to most people because they are unknown territory, but that also makes them a place of exploration, where new ideas reside. Step into this land of opportunity and you will be rewarded. Wherever we go and whatever we do, we inevitably hit bumps, turns, surprises and mysteries. Our journeys unfold in many different ways. Such is the fabric of life. Our organizational lives are the same way.

As leaders and managers, our work requires interface and connectivity to others. How we deal with obstacles and challenges is what makes the difference. Taking what we commonly think of as hard or uncomfortable moments with co-workers or subordinates and turning them into opportunities to explore, grow and be creative is the key to building solid relationships and getting work done well. Ignoring these opportunities to "reboot" our relationships will only lead to poor work and, possibly, a descent into more painful conflicts.

Exercises

Think of a time when you felt a pinch and ignored it. Describe the circumstances. What told you something was awry? What happened?

Think of a time you felt a pinch and attended to it successfully. What happened? What made it successful?

Scan your working situation now. Where do you see or

feel a "pinch"? Who or what has you worrying?

2 | The rebooting conversation

"It's not what you said, it's how you said it."
—Everyone I know

I don't know where that quote originated but I have heard that refrain a million times. I am sure you have as well. So how do you say what you want to say, and say it well? Let me review the steps of a rebooting conversation, and how to manage yourself while you are in it.

The steps:

1. Name the topic of the conversation.
2. Open with a genuine shared goal.
3. Ask the other person to share her perspective.
4. Share your perspective.
5. Ask for what you want.
6. Detail next steps, accountabilities and follow-up mechanisms.
7. Acknowledge the other person.
8. Do your part of the follow-up.

How to manage yourself:

1. Listen, listen, listen.
2. Be curious.

We've all heard the expression, "The devil is in the details." The steps are simple, but paying attention to the nuances is important.

In the following chapters I will describe each step in more detail and offer some exercises for you to try. Use this book in the way that works for you. If you feel you understand some of the steps, then skip those chapters and focus on the ones you don't understand or that you feel you may need to polish a bit.

I highly recommend doing the exercises and practicing the steps. If you have a particular situation in mind, you might try following the book in order and doing the exercises with that person in mind. This should prepare you very well for actually having the rebooting conversation.

You may also find yourself imagining different situations for different exercises. That will work as well. The important point is to DO the exercises, because it is through trying out these new skills that you will become proficient at them and be able to adapt them to your own style. Be willing to learn from each attempt.

Step 1
Name the topic

Calling someone into a meeting may raise the other person's anxiety, especially if you are the boss. When you first sit down together, it's important to explain the conversation you want to have. This gives context to the conversation and allows the other person to focus. Simply state, "I want to talk with you about...." Fill in that blank with neutral language, such as:

- *I want to talk about your weekly reports.*
- *I want to discuss how the project is coming along.*

The key is to name a topic without putting a negative spin on it. Just keep it factual.

Exercises

Think of a situation that you want to discuss with someone. It could be a general conversation or it might be a more serious topic. What is the subject?

What are the facts? What information do you have that tells you there is a problem or a need for a conversation?

Tip: Pretend that you are describing the situation to another person. You might use a piece of paper, a flip chart or a white board. Create a flow chat. Start with the first event, then note all subsequent events. Ask yourself:

- Do you have all the facts? What's missing?
- How did you contribute to the situation?
- What do you see as the other person's contribution? (Do not label with a judgment; keep it factual.)
- Now that you have all these details charted, what do you need to know to more fully understand the situation?
- What do you want to see happen differently?

Step 2
Offer a shared goal

How a conversation begins often foreshadows how it will end. Setting up the conversation well will increase the likelihood of a better outcome. This may be one of the most important steps. It is certainly the part I hear the most about from the managers and leaders to whom I have taught this technique.

A shared goal is a goal that you genuinely believe you have in common with the other person. The purpose of opening with a shared goal is to transmit to the other person that your intent is to help her, and that you have her interest at heart. If you can authentically let the other person know that you are concerned about her and her success, she is more likely to 1) relax, and 2) listen.

You may think you don't have a shared goal with some people, but you do. It's something both you and the other person want. Something that both of you will benefit from. The truth is that you, as a leader, cannot be successful without the success of your employees and co-workers. Their success is YOUR success. You have, intrinsically, a shared, overarching goal: the success of your group or organization. And you have many more shared goals. Here are some examples:

- *I want you to be successful here and I want to be successful as well.*
- *I want your project to go well.*
- *I am interested in helping to support your professional growth.*
- *I know you care about this effort or project; I would like to support you in seeing it to completion.*

If you are completely unable to find one genuine shared goal, enter the conversation by asking the other person what goals she has. You can begin by simply saying, "I want to get a better understanding of your career goals." Or, "What do you hope to be doing in the next five years?"

Many of my clients who have used this technique say that offering a shared goal disarmed people who entered defensive or scared, and that it opened the door to having a truthful, thoughtful conversation—which in turn led to solutions that both parties could agree to implement. My most skeptical clients were often the ones who were most surprised by the power of acknowledging a mutual, and mutually supportive, aim.

Exercises for identifying a shared goal

Think of someone with whom you want to have a potentially difficult conversation. Ask yourself:

- What does this person care about?
- What are this person's career aspirations?
- What skills, talents or attributes does this person possess?
- If this person were successful, what benefit would I receive?
- How does this person's work or function contribute to the work of the team, department or organization?

If you can answer any one of these questions, you have a goal. This person's desire to move up, or to be more successful at work, is easy to support. Again, this person's success is YOUR success. Find what the person wants and see how it links to your own success. That is a shared goal.

Additional exercises

Observe the person for one week with an intention of finding what she is doing well. Look for any contribution she makes that is positive. It could be a work product, a comment, an idea she offers, attention to time or simply a personal quality that impacts others positively. Often when we are in a negative mind frame about someone, we only look for the negative data. Try looking for the positive. You might be surprised.

Ask other co-workers to tell you three things that they really value about this person.

Step 3
Begin with the other person

Before you launch into your perspective, ask the other person to share how she sees things. Inviting her to speak early sends a message that you are going to listen to her and that, in a positive sense, you expect her to be a full participant in the conversation.

Allowing people to speak has three important effects. First, it often surprises them. This is a good thing. Most people enter a conversation like this defensively and assume there will be a need to explain, defend or fight. Asking them to speak creates an opening and space for them to express themselves. There is nothing to react to, and they feel no need to push back or defend. Nothing has been said to resist or argue with! Second, it signals that you are willing to take into consideration their thoughts, and that this is going to be a dialogue. Third, it models what you want them to do later in the conversation: listen. If you want them to listen to you,

you have to listen to them.

Let's pause to talk about listening. Listening isn't just letting words drift in one ear and then drift out the other. Nor is it about disputing or judging what is being said. Listening implies that you are genuinely interested in understanding the other person's perspective. It does NOT mean agreeing with the person. It simply means that you, for just this moment, are willing to step into the other person's shoes and see what the situation looks like to her.

Listening entails:

- Making eye contact and giving your full attention to someone (no interruptions!).
- Taking in the information (being receptive).
- Asking open-ended questions to explore more deeply (being curious).
- Repeating back to the person what you heard her say.

As the conversation unfolds and the other person speaks, be interested in her perspective. Ask questions for clarity and facts. Help the other person deliver to you the information she sees as important. Be curious, especially about what the situation looks like from the other person's perspective.

Asking open-ended questions is a very helpful tool because they cannot be answered with a simple "yes" or "no." They require explanation. Open-ended questions allow you to discover or explore what is happening for the other person.

Here are some examples of open-ended questions:

- *What are some of the challenges you face when you are trying to develop a timeline for your projects?*
- *What kinds of help do you need?*
- *What do you think is contributing to this problem?*
- *How do you think things are going?*
- *What process did you use to formulate that recommendation?*
- *What have you tried so far to improve the situation?*

Open-ended questions invite a broader understanding and often help people explore an issue for themselves. Just as questioning can give you a better understanding of a situation, the person with whom you're talking may, in fact, arrive at a new perspective just by being asked to expound a bit. Together you may be able to paint a picture that is more detailed and more accurate. Most importantly, you will each have a fuller picture.

The last step in the listening sequence—repeating back to someone what she has told you—cannot be overlooked. It does two very important things.

First, it verifies that you have correctly understood the message and that you and the other person have the same information. If you have the same information, and a shared understanding of the situation, you will then be able to move on to discovering solutions. If you have different information, you will not be able to arrive at a satisfactory solution because you may be trying to solve different problems!

Second, repeating back also ensures that the other person feels heard. When people feel heard, they feel valued and, in turn, they are more ready and able to listen to you. What more could you ask for? (A lot, I am sure, but for now, this is pretty good.)

Exercises to find open-ended questions

Practice asking open-ended questions. Any time during the day, with anyone of your choosing, start a conversation. Make it your goal to see if you can explain at the end of the conversation how the person sees the situation you have been discussing. You can try this with your spouse, a significant other, a friend, a child or a co-worker. Make it a game. Ask yourself, "What don't I know about this person that I would like to know?" And then go find out. Ask at the end if you got it right.

If you are planning to have a serious conversation with someone and you don't think you have any questions readily available, spend some time being curious. If you haven't already, write down what you think you know. You can also diagram the situation. Note all the players and what actions they are taking. Create a timeline of events. Then ask yourself where there are gaps in information, and what else you should know to have a fuller understanding of the problem or situation. What would help you figure out what is happening or determine a good remedy? If nothing comes, try explaining the situation to someone else. In the story telling, notice what you can't explain. There's a question.

Role-play. Take the part of the other person and ask someone to talk with you about the particular subject you want to broach. Listen to the questions you're asked. What helped?

Have a conversation with someone else and, at the end, ask that person to summarize what she heard. Notice the impact this has on you.

Use your thoughts and feelings, especially if they are negative, to lead you to a question. Do not ignore your feelings. They contain information. You need to think about what is causing them and you need to take some of the heat out of the situation if you are truly worked up. Recognizing how you are feeling actually lets you take one step back and observe. This alone can "unhook" you.

Some managers and leaders express reluctance to say what they are really experiencing because they are afraid they might lose control. This concern is quite common. Recognizing your feelings is not the same as acting on them. You don't have to act on them at all.

Allowing yourself to let your most negative thoughts surface so that you can listen to them will help you enter a conversation calmly and equipped with some initial questions.

So go ahead and try it. What would you really like to ask this person? Maybe it's something you feel is wrong to ask, like: "Are you nuts?" "Do you want to get fired?" "Have you been listening to me?" Let yourself brainstorm all those questions. What would you say if you didn't edit yourself? The essence of a more rational, thoughtful question is there. The trick is to turn those negative thoughts into helpful questions. First, ask the question. Then look at what the question is about. For example:

"Are you nuts?" In this question, you are asking about someone's thinking abilities. You might turn it in to, "What led you to take that action?"

"Do you want to get fired?" Here you are wondering about the person's motivation. An alternative might be, "How do you see yourself advancing here?" or "How do you feel about your work?"

"Haven't you been listening?" In this question you are again wondering about the person's ability to comprehend the situation, or maybe her motives. You could ask, "When I am trying to give you directions, what can I do to help you clearly understand them?" "What's the most effective way for me to communicate

with you?" Or, "You and I talked about this last week, and I am wondering, what happened that caused you to not follow through?"

Try some of your own. If you get stuck, ask a trusted friend to help you shape the question into something that can be delivered respectfully and that will help you and the other person explore together.

Step 4
Share your perspective

Once the other person has spoken, ask her if you might share your perspective. Then deliver a clear, thoughtful summation of how you are seeing the situation. In concrete, specific terms, explain its impact or why it's important. Allow the other person to ask questions, and ask her to summarize what she heard you saying. This will ensure that your message was delivered.

One key to this step is to describe the situation as factually as possible. What you say should be something a camera could capture on film. The facts should speak for themselves. You should avoid broad judgments as much as possible. People cannot necessarily change your opinion, but they can change their behavior. Telling someone she did a lousy job is not very helpful because it doesn't describe what exactly she did or what she needs to change or do differently. "There were 12 typos in this memo" or "You were 10 minutes late every day last week" are specific, factual statements. Someone hearing specific data or facts can then focus on what she needs to do differently.

This is also true in a positive situation. Telling someone she did a terrific job might feel good, but she will have no idea what exactly she did that made it terrific. How could she repeat it? For example, you could say, "When you spoke to that irate customer, you remained calm, used a quiet tone of voice and offered to follow up. I saw her calm down in response. That was a very effective way to handle someone who is upset. I believe she is more likely to stay a customer." This tells the person precisely what behaviors she demonstrated and their impact.

Another key when sharing your perspective is to be willing to take responsibility for what you see as your own contribution to the situation. What have you been doing to support the dynamics as they are now? How can you change your behavior to alter the dynamics? The answer to these questions is your key to making sure there is a change, because it gives you the power to reboot the dynamics in the relationship. (Think of a situation as a mobile with hanging parts; if you shift your piece of the mobile, the other parts move as well.)

Your contribution may be hard to find or easily recognizable. It might have been simply that you delayed in dealing with the issue, or that you didn't know there was a problem. It might have been an action such as being unclear, failing to respond or changing your mind. Whatever it is, it is. Simply be willing to see it and be willing to do something different.

Recognizing your contribution is also important because the adage, "Do as I say, not as I do," does not work. Your co-worker will not change if you won't. So your assumption of responsibility models the behavior you are requesting from the other person, and it sets up an expectation that the other person should take this process seriously.

Exercises

Think of someone with whom you want to have a conversation about improving work performance. What facts do you have? What has told you there is a problem? What have you seen? Heard? Experienced? If there had been a camera on this person, what would the camera have recorded? Are there any work measurements available, such as revenue, production numbers, days in accounts receivable or other empirical evidence that could show progress or success? Attempt to now describe the situation or your perspective using that information and data-based language.

Imagine again someone you would like to speak with about behavior or work performance. Imagine that your conversation went really well and the person was behaving exactly they way you had hoped. What would you be seeing? What would she be doing? Saying? What other data would you have?

Think about any situation. Ask yourself: What have I done to support this situation? In what ways did I either allow it to happen or actually contribute directly? If I could rewind the situation, what would I do differently? What could I do in the future to change this dynamic?

Think about how the other person might describe the situation. What does it look like from her perspective? What might she see as my contribution to the situation? What would she have liked me to do?

Step 5
Ask for what you want

Once you have shared how you see things, make a clear request or state what you want done. This is your opportunity to tell the other person what you need from her. You may have a request for a correction or remedy or you may want the other person to offer you a solution that will get you the change you are looking for. You may brainstorm ideas together and then select a solution together.

However you choose to do it, be sure the goal and the steps to achieve it are clear, specific, concrete and measurable. Saying, "I don't want you to be late anymore," may seem clear but it's not specific enough. Saying, "I want you here, at your desk and ready to work every day by 9:00 a.m. for the next 30 days," tells the person exactly what her behavior must look like to be considered, by you, as successful.

Engaging the other person in a negotiated solution is one of the best ways to get her buy-in and commitment to following through. As much as possible, invite the other person to offer her ideas or solutions. Sometimes, it may be necessary to ask her to propose a solution before you make any decisions or offer any ideas of your own. This may entail taking a break and giving the other person some time to prepare. That's fine. Tell the other person that you want her ideas for a plan of action that will get you the results YOU are looking for. Be sure that you set a follow-up time and stick to it.

Finally, be sure you can live with the agreement. Do not agree to anything that you cannot truly support.

At the conclusion of this step ask the other person to summarize what you have said and what you are expecting to happen next. This will verify that you have been heard and that she understands what is expected from her. It will show you that there is a shared understanding. If there isn't, revisit the agreement until it is clear to both of you.

Step 6
Plan for next steps and breaches of agreements

As the conversation ends it is essential that you make explicit who is doing what and when. Inevitably things happen and agreements need to be reevaluated, so you need to plan together how you will handle bumps or problems that arise. Set up a time or a series of times to check in and see how things are going. Monitoring progress is what will ensure ongoing success.

Many managers and leaders complain that people are not accountable or that things don't happen after solutions are decided. Making sure to do this step will greatly increase your success rate. You must specify what is to be done and how you will know it is being done. And most importantly, you have to be sure to check that it was done. Once you demonstrate that you are going to hold the other person accountable, she will start following through.

Exercises

At the end of any conversation, restate the next steps and ask, "How will I know this has been done?" This question is great for any conversation in which an action has been delineated—even in personal conversations. For example, let's say you and your friend or spouse have made plans to go away and you have decided that one of you will make the arrangements. You can say, "So you are going to call the travel agent and make all the plans by Friday. When will you let me know the itinerary?" You could also simply ask, "Can you e-mail me the plans by Friday at 5:00 p.m.?" Practice a few times in low-risk conversations and see what happens

In your work environment, build a discussion of next steps into your meetings. State the next steps, who will do them, when they will be completed and how you will know they were accomplished. You can also just build into the beginning of your meetings a follow-up to the last conversation or meeting. For example, "Let's review what we said we would do and see what we have accomplished."

In a rebooting conversation, it's best to set a time for a follow-up conversation. So as you end the meeting, simply say, "Let's get our calendars and set a time to review our progress on this matter."

Step 7
Acknowledge the other person

As you close the conversation, it is important to take a moment to acknowledge the other person and recognize what you have accomplished together.

Tell the other person what she did during the course of the conversation that you appreciated. Acknowledging her contribution sends a very strong message that you recognize and appreciate her efforts. This reinforces the motivation to do more of the behavior you noticed. The more specific you can be, the more likely it is that she will be able to repeat that behavior. Your acknowledgment will also serve to strengthen your relationship.

In return, the other person may offer a similar acknowledgement back to you. Accept it gracefully. Many people deflect good news or compliments. It's important to absorb the comment. You will have worked hard and you deserve appreciation, too. Allowing yourself a moment of feeling successful will build your own confidence in conducting honest and candid conversations. Lastly, the feedback you receive from the other person will give you clues as to what kinds of behaviors you can use effectively the next time.

When acknowledging someone, use the following guidelines:

- You should express genuine appreciation.
- The subject of the acknowledgement must be recognizable to the other person.
- The acknowledgement can be about behavior or attitude, but it must be specific.
- Deliver the acknowledgement deliberately. Do not rush it or try to skate by. Make sure it "lands."

Here are some examples:

- *I really appreciated how open you were to hearing my thoughts.*
- *Your ideas for next steps really moved us forward.*
- *Your willingness to commit to these agreements demonstrates to me your motivation to do well.*
- *I appreciate how honest you were as we discussed our individual contributions to this situation.*

This is an easy step to ignore, but do not skip over it or do it lightly. This is one of the payoffs for having stepped up and handled a situation. Your relationship will have improved, you will have agreed upon actions to move your goals forward and you must reward yourself and the other person for a job well done!

Exercises

Practice with anyone you choose. Watch the person during a meeting or other activity. Notice what she is doing or how she is behaving. What specifically does she do that helps the situation proceed smoothly or well? Tell her. Watch for her reaction. Did it register?

Ask someone to tell you one thing you did well after a meeting or another interaction. Ask her to be specific. Notice your own reaction. How did it feel? Were you uncomfortable or was it easy?

Think of a time when you worked hard and someone

acknowledged you. How did that feel? Were you motivated to try again? Conversely, think of a time your efforts were not acknowledged. How did that feel? How did that affect your motivation?

Step 8
Do your part

So what does it mean to do your part? At the end of the rebooting conversation you will set next steps and accountabilities. It is imperative that you take responsibility for doing whatever you agreed to do. That might be having a follow-up meeting or it might be more substantive. You may have agreed to support the other person by getting her resources or information. You might have agreed to talk with some other people or simply to mull something over. Whatever you said you would do, you MUST do it, and do it on time. If you don't, you send the message that you did not reboot!

At the very least, you must be sure to follow up. If you and the other person have agreed to some action, you have to make time to review the action or results. Setting up and conducting a follow-up meeting signals that the agreements will be taken seriously. Follow-up is also an opportunity to reinforce your goodwill and the continued success of your work together. If all parties have done their parts, the follow-up will strengthen your relationship and build momentum for more collaboration. If the agreements have not been kept, the follow-up meeting becomes an opportunity to explore the situation further and find other solutions. In either case, conducting a review session will support continued success for both your work and your relationship.

Exercises

Practice making agreements and then acknowledging that you have kept them. It might mean diligently writing e-mails or making quick calls to simply say, "Done."

In a rebooting conversation, make note of the agreements you have made and then create a system to remember to do your part. You can write it down in your calendar, put a sticky note on your computer— whatever works for you.

3 | Tips for maintaining the flow

Track the conversation and stay on topic. Too often people deflect difficult conversations. They can do this in a variety of ways: blaming, defending, changing the subject, going on about a long story with little relevance to the topic at hand. Watch for those shifts in subjects and politely steer the person back. You can acknowledge other topics that the person raises and note them for future discussion. Write those other topics down so the person sees that you have captured them, but stay on topic.

Remain objective. Picture yourself on the same side of the table with the other person, or actually sit next to her. Envision the problem as being on the wall and look at it together. Think about the problem or issue objectively, rather than being about the other person or you. Focus the conversation on an objective issue to be examined together.

Stay divergent—in exploration mode—as much as possible. Explore all facets of a situation before making any decisions. Avoid early solutions. Managers I have worked with have almost always jumped to conclusions before fully exploring a situation, its underlying causes or its possible solutions. When this happens, the solutions or agreements are inevitably not satisfactory and need to be revisited.

See conflict in terms of managing differences. If you respect differences, they can be used well and leveraged for everyone's benefit. Different viewpoints offer added information and a richer picture of a situation, and they create more possibilities for solutions.

Take a break. Research has shown that using some simple breakthrough techniques can help spark creativity. Herbert Benson and William Proctor, in their book *The Breakout Principle*, document the science and biology behind these techniques. Generally, the steps to reach a new understanding are:

1. Struggling with a situation.
2. Letting go.
3. Changing activities or shifting your attention and allowing your mind to work subconsciously.
4. Discovering a new idea or sharing an "aha moment".
5. Integrating a new way of thinking or approaching a situation.

The key is allowing your mind to struggle for a time with an issue, and then letting go to allow your body and mind to work at a subconscious level where new ideas are found.

In difficult situations, this might mean dividing a

hard or complicated conversation into two separate meetings, or taking a break in the middle of a meeting and inviting the participants to take a moment and reflect. You might also insert some kind of exercise into the meeting to shift attention for a short period of time. However you do it, creating an opportunity to disengage and relax will help the brain assimilate the data and find new ideas.

4 | Preparing for the conversation

How you enter the conversation will affect how it turns out. If you enter relaxed, objective, open and clear, you will transmit that to the other person and create an atmosphere conducive to dialogue.

Preparing for the conversation will allow you to enter it feeling more confident and relaxed. Use this book and its exercises to guide you through preparation. Or follow an abbreviated process by asking yourself these questions. Be concrete and specific:

- What has been happening?
- What data do you have? What data do you need?
- What goal do you share with this person?
- What strengths or positive value does this person bring?
- What has been this person's contribution to the issue?
- What has been your contribution to this situation?
- What do you want to see different?
- What are you willing to do to support this person?
- What's the worst thing that could happen in this meeting—and what will you do if that occurs?

Thinking about the worst thing that could happen as a

result of your conversation will help you plan a strategy for action in the event that it does, in fact, happen. Though these fears don't usually pan out, preparing for them will help you relax prior to entering the room.

It's equally important to give advance consideration to timing, setting and mood before inviting the person into a conversation. Arrange an appropriate meeting place, allow sufficient time, then request the meeting. The timing should be as close as possible to the event that triggered the conversation, the setting should be a neutral location to equalize the power dynamics and there should be enough time to adequately address the issues.

It's better to finish early than not have enough time, so allow more time than you actually think is needed. Typically this is roughly double the time you think the conversation might take!

5 | In Conclusion

Once you feel prepared, you are ready to follow the rebooting steps:

1. Name the topic of the conversation.
2. Open with a genuine shared goal.
3. Ask the other person to share her perspective.
4. Share your perspective.
5. Ask for what you want.
6. Detail next steps, accountabilities and follow-up mechanisms.
7. Acknowledge the other person.
8. Do your part of the follow-up.

If you follow these steps you will find yourself in a new conversation. One that will build trust and openness, and that will lead to better working relationships and better results. You CAN do this. And the more you do it, the easier it becomes.

Better yet, as people in your organization experience the new conversation, you may notice them using it as well. So by rebooting your own relationships, you may be helping to create a new, and more successful, way of working.

About the author

Marcia Feola, MHA, MCC, CPCC is a specialist in developing high performance executives, managers and leadership teams. For 30 years she has helped corporations, executives and individuals hone their skills and develop winning careers and businesses. She is the founding partner of PowerfulWork, a consulting firm that provides management and leadership coaching and training. She holds graduate degrees and professional postgraduate certification from George Washington University and Georgetown University, where she was co-director of the Facilitation and Organization Development Programs. She is a Master Certified Coach with advanced certification from the Coaches Training Institute and the International Coach Federation.

For more information visit www.powerfulwork.com

2868388

Made in the USA